YOUR KNOWLEDGE HAS

Bibliographic information published by the German National Library:

The German National Library lists this publication in the National Bibliography;
detailed bibliographic data are available on the Internet at http://dnb.dnb.de .

Imprint:

Copyright © 2018 GRIN Verlag
Print and binding: Books on Demand GmbH, Norderstedt Germany
ISBN: 9783668660908

This book at GRIN:

https://www.grin.com/document/416070

Josip Bilandzija

Aus der Reihe: e-fellows.net stipendiaten-wissen

e-fellows.net (Hrsg.)

Band 2714

The key Elements of communication jamming. How can intentional signal disorders be prevented?

GRIN Verlag

GRIN - Your knowledge has value

Since its foundation in 1998, GRIN has specialized in publishing academic texts by students, college teachers and other academics as e-book and printed book. The website www.grin.com is an ideal platform for presenting term papers, final papers, scientific essays, dissertations and specialist books.

Visit us on the internet:

http://www.grin.com/

http://www.facebook.com/grincom

http://www.twitter.com/grin_com

COMMUNICATIONS JAMMING

SEMINAR ASSIGNMENT WS 2017

Author: Josip Bilandzija
University of Applied Science Stuttgart
Course of studies: Business Information Systems (B.Sc.)
Module: Seminar

Date: 04.02.2018

TABLE OF CONTENTS

1 INTRODUCTION

This paper gives an insight into communications jamming from the topic area of information security. It was made in the context of a university preparation to consolidate academic writing and style. It is part of the module 'Seminar' of the University of Applied Science Stuttgart and it is a mandatory element to pass this module.

What is jamming? The theoretical principle behind it is the jamming of data transmission in general between a transmitter and a receiver. The practical principle defines however the exclusive jamming of the data receiver. At this point of transmission the signal is weakest and most open to attack (Graham 2011: 95). There are few ways to attack the data exchange between two wireless connected points. First, the attacker is just passively listening and trying to conclude information. Second, the attacker is transmitting energy to disrupt dependable data transmission. Third, the attacker threatens integrity and confidentiality of a transmission on a higher-layer active attack. This writing describes attacks threatening availability, intended as Denial of Service (Dos) which affect one to more users at once (Lichtman et al.: 1).

We are able to split the whole topic off jamming into two parts of application. You can have a look at civilian use like radio station jamming, satellite TV stations jamming, Internet jamming, or mobile jamming, or you can have a look at military use like radar jamming or communications jamming (Haseeb 2015: 11). This assignment is going to describe the key elements of communications jamming, how it was used in history, how the general definition has changed over time, how it is described as jamming in the sense of wireless communications, and how to prevent against this kind of intentional signal disorders.

The key difference between interference and jamming is that interference is an unintentional radio disorder and jamming is an intentional radio noise, created so that the receiver cannot get required information. Jamming is a technique in which a receiver is overloaded with high power transmission of jamming signals from a jammer medium. The jammer itself is a transmitter (Haseeb 2015: 2-4). Jamming addresses the principle of timeliness. It does not impact the exchange of data directly, rather it is slowing it down. Time can be crucial especially if actual and timely information is needed at the destination, i.e. for tactical purposes in times of war. Jamming is not absolute, there exist still ways from which communication can take place (Poisel 2011: 2).

2 JAMMING – ELECTRONIC WARFARE

Radio frequency or communication jamming are based on disrupting communication of a specific radio object or satellite to disrupt the receiving or decoding at the receiving target. It was theoretically invented at the dawn of radio communication. This concept was born through military approaches during times of war to prevent interruption and interception of their radio transmission by enemy. The practical purpose of jamming is to prevent enemy from using radio link freely. Radio frequency jammers were used to jam near border areas by military (RF Wireless World). During World War Two the Nazis have used the concept to jam broadcast to Europe from allied stations. This idea was striding ahead through the Cold War era, Vietnam War and Arab-Israeli wars. During Cold War the eastern block was jamming some western, anti-communist broadcast satellites (Haseeb 2015). Satellite jamming is still in practice. In places where satellites are the only transmission node for information access, satellite jamming becomes a strong political tool, i.e. in Iran (A Small Media Report 2012).

2.1 DEFINITION OF JAMMING DURING THE COLD WAR ERA

Jamming in the era of Cold War was defined depending on its primary application. They were grouped into two general classes. One is the ground-wave or local jammer, located in cities and other heavily populated areas. This type of jammer was designed and situated as to interfere with reception in the immediate closeness by laying down a blanket noise with very high intensity but limited range. The other classification was grouped into sky-wave or long-range jamming. This included satellite transmission to cover large and distant areas.

A typical local jammer was consisting of from one to several dozen low-powered transmitters (about a few hundred to a few thousand watts) with antenna systems designed for maximum ground-wave coverage. Long-range jammers on other hand had relatively high-powered transmitters (about a few thousand to a few hundred thousand watts) with directional antenna systems to focus radiation on the target (RFE archive document 1965).

3 JAMMING – WIRELESS NETWORK

Jamming in the sense of wireless security or wireless networks is defined as disruption of an existing wireless transmission or communication by decreasing the signal-to-noise ratio at receiver side through transmission of interfering wireless signals. A signal-to-noise ratio (SNR or S/N) is the relationship between signals to background noise or rather background interferences. To understand how a jamming attack in this sense is defined, the different types of existing jammers have to be described before to build a basic acknowledge to create a concept for prevention (Int. J. Ad Hoc and Ubiquitous Computing: 1).

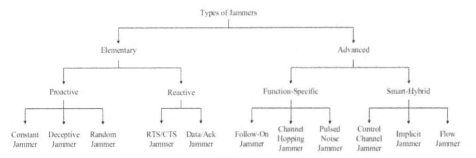

FIGURE 1: TYPES OF JAMMERS (SOURCE: INT. AD HOC AND UBIQUITOUS COMPUTING: 3)

3.1 TYPES OF JAMMERS

It exists a wide range of jammers, i.e. proactive, reactive, function-specific, or smart-hybrid jammers as shown in figure 1. In general, jamming uses intentional radio interferences to harm and disrupt wireless data transmission by keeping the transmission object busy as shown in figure 2. It backs-off the transmitter whenever it senses a busy wireless object or a corrupted signal received at target.

The jamming effectiveness depends on its radio transmitting power, its location and its influence on the wireless network or the target's node. A jammer can be either an elementary constant source of continuous wave interference or an advanced, intelligent jammer depending upon its functionality (Int. J. Ad Hoc and Ubiquitous Computing: 2).

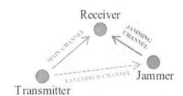

FIGURE 2: THREE CHANNELS OF JAMMING (SOURCE: LICHTMAN: 3)

3.1.1 ELEMENTARY TYPES

Now we are having a short look at the basic two sub-types of elementary jammers, proactive and reactive, and the two advanced sub-types, function-specific and smart-hybrid. In general, proactive jammers are interfering whether or not there is data transmission between transmitter and receiver. They are only working on one specific communication channel without switching until its energy is exhausted. They are sending packets or random bits to switch all the other nodes on this channel into non-operating ones. Depending on their proactive sub-type, as shown in figure one, they're easy to implement but inefficient in energy and effectiveness, and easy to prevent and localize. Against that, reactive jammers are only operating when they detect a network activity on certain channel. As soon as they sense a transmission, they harm the reception of the message (Int. J. Ad Hoc and Ubiquitous Computing: 2).

The advantages compared to proactive jammers are that they are more difficult to detect and more energy efficient. To conclude, the attributes, i.e. efficiency, detection, or prevention of both types of elementary jamming are depending of their specific sub-type as shown in figure one.

3.1.2 INTELLIGENT TYPES

Intelligent or advanced jammers are so called because of their energy efficiency and effectiveness advantage compared to elementary jammers. Their goal is to increase their jamming effect in the whole network they are working in. Next to the magnification, they are taking care of themselves by saving energy by placing sufficient energy in the right place. Intelligent jammers are working in multi-channel networks by targeting the control channel, causing denial-of-service (DoS) states, identifying weak access point, or/and involving multiple jammers. There is no strict specification for a divided use of elementary or advanced jamming methods, moreover both could be combined together (Int. J. Ad Hoc and Ubiquitous Computing: 3, 4).

4 JAMMER RELATIONS – DISTINCTION OF MAJOR CLASSES OF JAMMING

4.1 Radar Jamming

In times of war the enemy party wishes on one hand to get information about the other side, e.g. using radar systems. On the other hand the enemy party wishes to prevent their own tactical information so that the other side does not get them by usage of their radar systems. There are several countermeasure methods which might be used to accomplish these efforts, i.e. interception, deception, or jamming. We're just continuing with the description of radar jamming.

Radar jamming includes the production of strong signal to hide one's movements or positions from the enemy's radar by obliterating or confusing the radar transmissions, as shown in figure 3. The jamming transmitters might be carried by any military vehicle, i.e. aircrafts, ships, or any other ground vehicle. The transmitter is working on the enemy's radar frequency channel and has to be, as described before, stronger than the radar signal (maritime.org 2013: 3-25, 3-26).

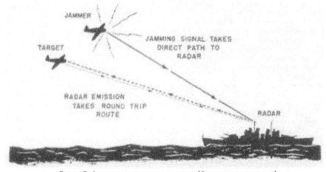

FIGURE 3: ILLUSTRATION OF RADAR JAMMING (SOURCE: MARITIME.ORG)

4.2 Radio Navigation Jamming

Radio navigation jamming includes the hiding of GPS tracking signals. In civilian use it should avoid tracking or monitoring of movements or positions by someone else using GPS. In military use it should i.e. avoid tracking or monitoring of movements or positions by the enemy, or it should i.e. confuse GPS coordinated missiles to miss their target.

4.3 COMMUNICATIONS JAMMING

4.3.1 KEY JAMMER CAPABILITIES

A jammer might have one or more of the following capabilities: Time correlation, protocol-awareness, ability to learn, signal spoofing. A time correlated jammer signal is depending on the target's signal in time. The jammer can alternately or simultaneously receive and send signals, signalize its own erase or use separate antennas. This means that a time correlated jammer has to be tightly synchronized to the target signal. To ensure capability the jammer has to be signal aware, threat analysing, and attack selecting. Signal awareness is the sensing and detecting of signals across the spectrum of interest. Threat analysing is the jamming decision making for each signal. Attack selection is the attack selection for each signal (Buehrer: 2, 3).

A protocol aware jammer is aware of the protocol of the target signal, in other words the jammer is identifying the specific signal protocol and might adjust its attack on this information to increase its efficiency, i.e. by jamming a physical layer mechanism (Buehrer: 3). A jammer, that has the ability to learn, is modifying itself by experience, not by coded instructions. The jammer may modify its behaviour in real-time but this is limited by following pre-coded sequences of change (Buehrer: 3, 4). A jammer which uses spoofing is able to masquerade itself as another by falsifying data or signals in order to gain illegitimate advantage. This means the jammer is sending signals which meant to look like legitimate signals (Buehrer: 4).

5 PHYSICAL LAYER OF JAMMING ATTACKS

We're now having a short look at the physical layer of jamming and how it works practically. To unfold this topic it must be described what radio frequency (RF) jamming basics are. First, the frequency of the jammer has to be equal to the target frequency, which has to be disrupted. Second, the modulation type of both has to be equal. Modulation is a process modifying a carrier signal to enable a high-frequency transmission of the low-frequency carrier signal (Homayounour 2012). Third, the power of the jammer has to be higher than the target's (RF Wireless World).

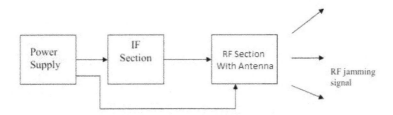

FIGURE 4: MOBILE JAMMER BLOCK DIAGRAM (SOURCE: RF WIRELESS WORLD: RF JAMMER BASICS)

A jammer, in general, consists of three parts as shown in figure 4. The first is the power supply, second the interference (IF) section, which generates the interference frequency, and third the radio frequency section with antenna, which converts the IF frequency into the RF frequency by using up converter. After that it's amplified using RF power amplifier and transmitted using RF antenna (RF Wireless World).

6 JAMMING ATTACK PREVENTION

Why to prevent jamming and why is it prohibited? As mentioned in the previous sections, jammers can block all radio communications. This includes mobile phones, any wireless Internet device, or satellite connections within the jammer's range by preventing establishing or maintaining a connection (FCC 2012: 2). A jammer generally does not differentiate between desirable or undesirable communication. For example, in case of an emergency you are not able to communicate to anyone, including emergency numbers like police. Or if someone activates a jammer insight a bigger stock market, the financial damage might skyrocket.

One simple concept of jammer prevention is to use multiple frequencies and to change them randomly. This can avoid disruption by simple elementary jamming types (Int. J. Ad Hoc and Ubiquitous Computing: 1). Another simple solution is to increase transmission power on jammed channels. The point, the transmitter power overcomes the jamming signal, is known as burn-trough. The result of this method is usually a power-race, so it is not always recommended (Haseeb 2015). However, none of the existing methods can prevent jamming attacks entirely.

7 SUMMARY AND CONCLUSION

As the wireless communication is becoming even more and more popular, communication jamming, or jamming in general, is becoming more significant as well. In civilian view, we like to be linked up in real-time and on every place and if something is disrupting this kind of freedom we might feel threatened. We should be seriously aware of jamming because an intentionally break down of signal communication in the wrong moment could have bad consequences, as described in this paper. In the military view, communication jamming is a very interesting way of protecting themselves from an enemy. This is a part of IT security, into which further research pays off.

But research is still lacking in terms of effective protection against jamming. There is currently no method that really completely protects against a jamming attack. We have to extent the jamming knowledge to achieve better jamming effects. This give us the opportunity to decrease the power of jammers by tactically placing them in the interference ranges of communicating nodes.

LIST OF SOURCES

A Small Media Report: *Satellite Jamming in Iran: A War over Airwaves*, Creative Commons Attribution-Non-commercial-ShareAlike, 2012, [online] https://smallmedia.org.uk/sites/default/files/Satellite%20Jamming.pdf [04.02.2018].

RFE archive document: *A History of Jamming*: DLW, 1965, [online] http://www.radiojamming.puslapiai.lt/doc/1601.jpg [04.02.2018].

Graham, Adrian: *Communications, Radar and Electronic Warfare*: 1st ed. John Wiley & Sons Ltd., United Kingdom, 2011, [online] http://ready4itall.org/wp-content/uploads/2013/05/Communications-Radar-Electronic-Warfare-2011.pdf [04.02.2018].

Lichtman, Marc; Poston, Jeffrey; Amuru, SaiDhiraj; Shahriar, Chowdhury; Clany, T. Charles; Buehrer, R. Michael; Reed, Jeffrey: *A Communications Jamming Taxonomy*, Blacksburg, Virginia, USA: Wirless(at)VT, Virginia Tech, [online] http://www.buehrer.ece.vt.edu/papers/Com_Jam_Taxonomy.pdf [04.02.2018].

Poisel, Richard: *Modern Communications Jamming: Principles and Techniques*: 2nd revised ed. Artech House, Norwood, 2011.

Haseeb, Abdul: *Presentation of Jamming*, 2015, [online] https://de.slideshare.net/AbdulHaseeb54/presentation-on-jamming [01.12.2017].

Int. J. Ad Hoc and Ubiquitous Computing (n.Y.): *Jamming and Anti-jamming Techniques in Wireless Networks: A Survey,* [online] https://www.cs.montana.edu/yang/paper/jamming.pdf [04.02.2018].

maritime.org: *OPERATION OF MAJOR TYPES OF RADAR*, 2013, [online] https://maritime.org/doc/radar/part3.htm#pg25 [04.12.2017].

Homayounpour, M. Mehdi; Mehralian, M. Amin; Valipour, M. Hadi, Tehran, Iran: *Automatic digital modulation recognition in presence of noise using SVM and PSO*: IST, 2012, [online] http://www.academia.edu/3100439/Automatic_digital_modulation_recognition_in_presence_of_noise_using_SVM_and_PSO [04.02.2018].

Federal Communications Commission: *FCC Enforcement Advisory – Call jammers, GPS jammer, and other jamming devices*, 2012, Washington, D.C., USA, [online] https://transition.fcc.gov/eb/Public_Notices/DA-12-347A1.html [04.02.2018].

RF Wireless World: RF Jammer basics, [online] http://www.rfwireless-world.com/Terminology/rf-jammer [02.12.2017].